NEW HOPE FOR ALCOHOLISM RECOVERY:
BEAT THE BOTTLE

I0439495

FOR MY MOTHER. FOR GIVING HER THE COURAGE TO STAY SOBER.

© 2012 BILL FROST

TABLE OF CONTENTS

INTRODUCTION

1. THE EFFECTS OF ALCOHOL ON THE HUMAN BODY

1.1 Short Term Effects of Alcohol
1.2 Long Term Effects of Alcoholism
1.3 The Liver
1.4 The Brain
1.5 The Stomach and Esophagus
1.6 The Immune System

2. RECOGNIZING ALCOHOLISM

3. DENIAL

4. DO YOU LOVE OR KNOW SOMEONE WHO IS AN ALCOHOLIC?

5. SEEKING HELP

6. DETOXING

7. TREATMENT

7.1 Faith based treatment
7.2 Inpatient Treatment Centers
7.3 Outpatient Therapy
7.4 Do It Yourself

8. CHANGING THE EMPHASIS FROM TREATMENT TO RECOVERY

9. THE RECOVERY PLAN: LIFE AFTER ALCOHOLISM

RECAP

LIMITED BONUS

INTRO

We live in a culture that makes drinking not only acceptable, but very attractive. In the media we see images of beautiful people drinking all the time and we see happy groups having a great time with drinks in their hands. Drinking has become synonymous with fun and great times. When a person drinks too much, people are generally more than willing to accept that it is an occasional blunder and simply let it pass. While it is true that some people can drink occasionally and enjoy themselves while not overindulging, there are many people who are not capable of doing that. These are the people who become problem drinkers and alcoholics.

Why does this happen? No one really knows. Some researchers have tried to point to a genetic reason for why some people can drink without problems and others cannot, some have tried to find environmental influences that make some people lose control of how much they drink, and some people have tried to blame moral character. The simple truth is, we do not really understand why some people can drink or even do drugs without any negative effects and others can become full-blown alcoholics or drug addicts, practically overnight. If you are a problem drinker or alcoholic or you care about someone who is, the reasons behind the problem do not mean anything when you awake in the morning with the shakes and feel like you are going to explode if you don't get a drink or if you are on your way downtown to bail someone out of jail for the latest Driver Under Influence (DUI). Once a drinking problem becomes serious enough to require intervention, stopping the destructive behavior is all that matters.

When the stock market falters, the stocks of beer and spirits seldom even quiver. Alcohol is very big business in the US and around the world. Alcoholism is a major problem in the United States. Over 15 million people either have a serious drinking problem or are affected by someone who does. 14% of teenagers report that they have been intoxicated at least once. In 2009 1.4 million people were arrested for DUI's. This all sounds pretty staggering, and you would think this information would open people's eyes, but people keep ruining their lives and the lives of others around them by continuing to abuse alcohol. Alcoholics either refuse to believe they have a problem or feel the problem cannot be solved so they continue with the status quo until time runs out; for them or someone else.

The good news is that there have been major changes in treatment in the last 20 years and today, recovery from alcoholism is a very real and obtainable outcome, for just about every alcoholic. New techniques and a better understanding of addiction (yes, alcoholism is an addiction) and treatment has made overcoming alcoholism a realistic goal. It is still a tough road to walk and some painful decisions still need to be made, but knowing that there really is a proverbial light at the end of the tunnel, can make all the difference in the world.

There are five main stages to addiction treatment and recovery:

1. **Recognition of the problem**

2. **Seeking help**

3. **Detox and abstinence**

4. **Treatment**

5. **Recovery**

This book will discuss these five areas of treatment and recover, the physical effects of alcoholism on the human body and also the effects on loved ones, friends and colleagues and the responsibilities of each when involved with a person who is suffering an addiction. We hope that after reading this book you will have a better understanding of alcoholism, its treatments and the potential for continued recovery.

There is more hope now for recovery from alcoholism and other addictions than ever before.

<u>Note</u>: Throughout this book, the terms, "alcoholic" and "addict" will be used interchangeably.

CHAPTER 1
THE EFFECTS OF ALCOHOL ON THE HUMAN BODY
1.1 Short Term Effects of Alcohol

Consuming alcohol in moderation is not considered a problem, but what exactly is, "moderation?" When it comes to what the standard blood alcohol level is, in the US, for driving under the influence, the percentage is quite low; since 2011, the US standard is 0.08% alcohol blood level (0.04 for commercial drivers). This can mean, for a 130 pound woman, three drinks and for a 150 pound man, as little as four drinks and then it becomes illegal to drive a vehicle. The time limit for blood levels to begin to return to normal is considered four hours after the last drink for most people and eight hours for commercial drivers.

What happens to the body as the number of drinks increases and the blood alcohol levels rises? The higher the blood level, the more impaired a person becomes. As the blood level of alcohol increases, the person moves from feeling joyous and euphoric to having decreased inhibitions. The next stage is having emotional swings, and severe motor impairment. If the person continues to drink, he or she will eventually move into a stage of blackout drinking (forgetting what has happened while drunk) and ultimately into losing consciousness, which can result in lowered body functions and even death.

People who pass out from drinking can choke to death if they vomit while being unconscious and, if a person has consumed a very high amount of alcohol so quickly that the body continues to absorb the alcohol after becoming unconscious, the person's body functions can slow to the point that the person dies. This is called death by alcohol poisoning. If someone loses consciousness because of excessive drinking, that person should be placed on his or her side to prevent the possibility of choking and vital signs should be carefully monitored. There is a big difference between falling asleep and losing consciousness and anytime a person loses consciousness, there is a potential danger of serious medical problems or death occurring.

College students and people at parties have been known to consume large quantities of alcohol very quickly as a part of games or dares (also known as binge drinking) and this sudden, large amount of alcohol that the body cannot properly absorb can cause sudden death. This is a very real danger that many people are not aware of and the result can and often is fatal simply because no one knew it could happen

1.2 Long Term Effects of Alcoholism

There are some subtle signs of alcoholism to look for that show up when a person is consuming too much alcohol for the body to properly handle. Many of these signs are symptoms of other problems, but when several of them show up at one time, there is a good possibility that the person is an alcoholic. The skin around the nose and mouth will become redder than usual and for people with light complexions you can even see broken blood vessels under the skin on the face. The eyes are frequently red or bloodshot, and there will be dark puffy areas under them. People frequently become a bit puffy all over, particularly on the face, and the skin on the face and neck begins to prematurely sag.

1.3 The Liver

Chronic alcohol use can have profound effects on the human body. The body was not designed to deal with large amounts of alcohol at one time and especially not for prolonged periods of time. The liver simply cannot deal with the amount of alcohol that passes through it to be detoxified and begins to have serious problems like fatty liver, cirrhosis of the liver, alcoholic hepatitis and even cancer of the liver. Some of these medical issues can be reversed once a person stops consuming alcohol, but liver disease is one of the most common medical reasons for death among alcoholics.

1.4 The Brain

Brain damage is one of the most profound lasting ill effects of alcoholism. The sad truth about brain damage is that most of it is permanent; the brain does not have the capability to replace dead cells like other parts of the body can. The brain can sometimes use other areas that are not as damaged to learn to take the place of the destroyed areas, but once brain cells have been killed in large quantities, they are never going to be replaced. The brain is not like a bone or the skin that can heal itself with time; it does not produce new cells that take the place of dead ones. There have been several people in the news lately whose alcoholism has been made very public, especially when they have shown up for interviews intoxicated or in a mental condition that has made them appear intoxicated. These people are living, public proof that large amounts of alcohol can kill brain cells in such high numbers as to cause permanent brain damage. People who once appeared intelligent, begin to lose the ability to learn new facts or recall information that was once stored in the memory and become forgetful and easily irritated.

1.5 The Stomach and Esophagus

The stomach lining and the lining of the esophagus can be severely damaged by alcohol. Some people can have this happen in a very short period of time and start to have problems with indigestion and ulcers with even moderate amounts of alcohol. Many alcoholics have bled to death when ulcers which have formed in the stomach or esophagus have ruptured. You cannot put a tourniquet or a pressure dressing on internal bleeding. Once internal bleeding starts, it is a very desperate matter of life and death.

1.6 The Immune System

When the body has to spend so much time trying to cope with the effects of chronic, large amounts of alcohol, it cannot renew itself or heal itself enough to be able to deal with the other problems that we face, every day. Colds, viruses, germs and other diseases are always around that the body must fight off and of course there are cuts, bruises, and other injuries that require the body to work hard to heal or cure. A body that must spend all of its energy fighting off the effects of alcohol does not have the resources left to fight off anything else. The person who consumes large amounts of alcohol begins to age prematurely, is likely to start getting more and more common illnesses that last longer and cause more damage than usual and simply cannot fight off diseases. Many chronic alcoholics die from diseases like pneumonia or infections that most people can easily fight off. If you think of the body as having just a certain amount of energy and resources to deal with everyday problems and then you add dealing with large amounts of a substance like alcohol on a daily basis, you can begin to understand why systems begin to fail and to break down and the result is frequently premature death.

CHAPTER 2
RECOGNIZING ALCOHOLISM

Do you or someone you love or know have a drinking problem? Is it serious enough to require some kind of intervention? Sometimes a person only needs to recognize that his or her drinking has gotten out of hand and this recognition is enough to get things back to a healthy level. Unfortunately, for many people, recognizing that there is a problem is simply the first step in a process that can ultimately result in recovery. So, let's take a look at some of the signs and symptoms of alcoholism and see if there is a problem that needs intervention. Can you honestly answer "yes" to at least half of these questions or know someone who can?

Do you …

Ever feel guilty about drinking or tell lies about how much alcohol you have consumed?

Need a drink to relax, unwind, or feel better and may feel jittery or nervous without one?

Need a drink in the morning to stop shaking or to feel well enough to function?

Feel like you have lost control of how much you drink?

Think you would like to cut down or quit drinking but are afraid that you can't?

Give up other activities because of drinking?

Have at least one DUI?

Ever go to work intoxicated?

Or…

Has drinking caused you to have trouble sleeping?

Has drinking ever caused you to have financial problems?

Have you ever had a loss of memory due to drinking (known as a blackout)?

Have you ever become violent when drinking?

Do your family members or friends worry about your drinking?

Any person who can answer "yes" to even half of these questions, is an alcoholic who requires intervention.

CHAPTER 3
DENIAL

One of the biggest obstacles (that most alcoholics live with) to recognizing alcoholism in yourself, is the denial that prevents alcoholics from seeing how much of a problem alcohol has become. You may be underestimating the amount of alcohol you consume. You may be minimizing the problems alcohol is causing. You may think that your family and friends are exaggerating the problems; you may even be blaming others for your drinking. The truth is, you are lying to yourself and others about the seriousness of your drinking and how much of a problem it is causing in your life.

Why do people deny the problems? If you face the truth about the need to stop drinking, it is going to be very scary. You know, deep down, that this is going to mean a huge change in your life that is going to be extremely unpleasant and you are not 100% certain if the results are going to be worth it. One of the biggest fears faced by all alcoholics is that, in the end, their life is going to be lonely and unhappy if they are not drinking. Some alcoholics think they would rather die than face that void.

An alcohol abuse counselor will tell you that it is the "alcohol talking" when you have those kinds of feelings. It is the addiction trying to convince you that you cannot be happy if you stop drinking. Drug addicts and alcoholics both have this problem and it is the hardest, toughest hurdle to get over when thinking about recovery. It is, quite literally, like the alcohol has turned you into a con artist who is conning yourself! The thought of quitting is so scary that you have convinced yourself that you cannot do it and if you do, it will make your life miserable. Until you can overcome this fear, you will not quit.

Many alcoholics or addicts must get to the point called "hitting the bottom" before they are finally willing to give up the addiction. This is a point in your life where things have gotten so bad that the choice becomes to quit or die and the person chooses not to die.

You do not have to get that far down to make the decision to quit. There are many good things in life that you can enjoy after you have recovered. There is still a lot of joy to be had and finally, recovery has become a real possibility. New discoveries have changed our understanding of addiction and alcoholism in the last few years and this means treatment has improved and people are learning that they really can completely recover from alcoholism. Life after alcoholism can be joyful, happy and fulfilling. It can be full of love and many of the things that have been passing you by. Your life can once again be truly yours and not that of a ruined person who allows alcohol to make every decision for you.

Why you drink or why you first started drinking does not matter at this point. If drinking started out as a form of coping, self medicating, or a good time that got out of hand, the drinking has become a major problem itself and no longer serves its original intention. Many of us start drinking to feel better, less lonely or less depressed or less disappointed; somewhere along the way, the drinking became the problem instead of the cure. The original problem may or may not still be a part of your life, but alcoholism has taken its place as being the major obstacle to happiness or self fulfillment.

CHAPTER 4
DO YOU LOVE OR KNOW SOMEONE WHO IS AN ALCOHOLIC?

If you know or love someone who is a problem drinker or alcoholic, there is actually very little you can do to help. That sounds pretty cold or pessimistic, but only the drinker can make the decision to quit drinking. He or she must decide that quitting is important and want to do it. If a person is forced to seek treatment, either by the courts or by someone who is trying to help, the alcoholic is going to be angry and resentful.

You can scream and cry, you can take away the car keys (if the law hasn't already), you can make threats, but that is not going to solve anything. The best thing you, as a friend, loved one or family member can do is to remove yourself from the situation, as much as possible. Living with or caring about an alcoholic is so difficult that you must first make sure that you take care of yourself. While this, again, sounds cold or impossible, the alcoholic is the only one who can decide to seek help and all you can do is get hit by the fallout until that happens. The alcoholic is incapable of taking care of anyone else and only cares about him or herself.

Living with or caring about an alcoholic can be very painful; if a person's drinking has gotten out of control enough that the problems are piling up, you will not help by covering up for him or her. Every time you do something that makes it acceptable or easy to drink, you are helping him or her put off the inevitable, a little bit longer. This is known as "enabling", it means that you are actually helping the person to continue drinking by enabling him or her to get away with it. The alcoholic has no reason to quit drinking if you are making it possible to keep at it. The alcoholic needs to come to the decision to quit the destructive behavior by his or herself and want to do it for that same reason. That is when the decision will mean something and help can be found.

If you are involved with or living with a person who becomes violent when drinking, you need to leave and find help. There are shelters in almost every city that can offer you safety from abuse. Alcoholics who become violent do not realize how much they are hurting the other person or how violent they really are. A violent alcoholic can cause you serious injury or even kill you and never remember it happening or understand how it happened at all. If you are involved with an alcoholic who becomes violent, you are in grave danger. If you have not left yet, please do so or at least always have a charged cell phone with you: even cell phones that have no minutes left will connect you with 911.

You are not alone. There are groups like Al-Anon for people who are involved with alcoholics and they are easy to find in the phone book or online. There are also hotlines to call. Just about every program that has been created to help alcoholics can either help friends or family members of alcoholics or refer you to someone who can. Remember: you can call 911 at any time, even from a cell phone with no minutes left, and be referred to someone who can help.

There is no need to deal with the heartbreak of loving or caring about an alcoholic, alone; there are people who are waiting for you to contact them so that they can help.

CHAPTER 5
SEEKING HELP

Once you have recognized that you have a problem, you do not have to face it alone. There are decisions to be made and many other things that require action and knowledge and all of that can seem overwhelming. There is a lot of help available to answer your questions and help you to decide exactly what direction you want to move in. Help is as close as your telephone or computer.

The easiest way to get help and answers to your questions is simply to open your phone book and look in the social services area or even the government offices in the front of the book. You can look up counseling or even alcoholism or addiction in the yellow pages. You can do the same thing online. There are many alcohol hotlines that you can call to get help and information. Do not call just one; talk to several experts and weigh what they have to say. When you find someone you are truly comfortable talking to, then you have taken an important step in getting help. Remember: if someone asks you for money, hang up! There is plenty of free help available and if you chose to enter any type of treatment that has a fee, that must be your decision, but only a decision that has been made after you have had a chance to put all of the facts together and are able to make an informed decision. Remember: There are dishonest people and companies online and you must be ready to recognize these. Anyone who asks you for money before beginning to help you or provide good, solid information is probably scamming you. If you say you need time to decide what you want to do and are suddenly pressured to make an immediate decision, you are most likely not talking to a reliable source. Always ask for references that you can check yourself before putting your welfare in someone's hands.

CHAPTER 6
DETOXING

Some people chose to tackle their problems on their own, some chose to see a counselor or therapist on an outpatient basis and some people chose to enter a hospital or residential program. The choice is up to you and we will discuss those options in the next chapter. If you are addicted to alcohol, quitting can mean detoxing (short for detoxification). This means that when the alcohol is leaving your system (much like having a toxic substance leaving your system), there can be medical problems. Many people can experience withdrawal at home with mild symptoms that include headache, some tremors, nausea and irritability. Some people will have more moderate symptom that include vomiting, sweating, loss of appetite and severe aches and pains. A person who has been consuming large amounts of alcohol for a long period of time can experience severe withdrawal symptoms such as seizures and even death.

It is always best to consult a physician before withdrawing from Alcohol or any drug. A physician can prescribe medications that can make the withdrawal symptoms much more manageable or recommend hospitalization if it appears the symptoms could become serious. Hospitals and special detox centers are well equipped to deal with any and all medical problems that can occur during the process of withdrawal. There is no reason for a person to suffer during withdrawal from alcohol or any other drug. Gone are the days when someone expected an alcoholic or addict to detox without medication to help with symptoms. Wherever you live, there are hospitals or treatment centers that can help you to stop drinking without painful symptoms. Many people even sleep through the initial phases of detox.

Being hospitalized during detox is not the same as being in treatment, although it can and is part of many treatment centers' initial therapy. Many people are hospitalized for only two to three days to complete the initial detox treatment and then go on to other programs or simply return home to receive therapy on an outpatient setting or to recover on their own. While in detox, a social welfare or alcohol rehabilitation specialist will generally visit the patient to discuss therapeutic options that are available.

CHAPTER 7
TREATMENT

This discussion of treatment options will start with the most structured and moves to the least structured. The majority of alcoholics and addicts can benefit most from a structured, inpatient setting. This is a great opportunity to be away from alcohol and the places where you normally drink and to learn more about alcoholism, why you drink and what triggers cause you to drink. You can also make plans for maintaining your recovery after discharge.

7.1 Faith based treatment

One form of treatment is called faith based or Spiritual based and many of these centers use Christian based counseling and therapy to help their patients. These treatment centers have a high rate of success, and because many of them are supported by churches, they can accept church members who have limited funds. Most faith based treatment centers now use very modern philosophies and treatment techniques. These treatment centers do not place blame or use sin as a threat. While some more conservative centers may continue to use those techniques, most now realize that treating addiction as an illness has been the most successful form of treatment, worldwide. Why these Faith based treatment centers have a high success rate will be explained in a later chapter.

7.2 Inpatient Treatment Centers

Most modern inpatient treatment centers use a combination of methods and it is this combination that seems to help many people to maintain sobriety after discharge. This combination generally consists of one-on-one psychotherapy, group counseling, a form of treatment called Cognitive Behavioral Therapy (CBT) and family therapy, if appropriate. Most also use some form of the Alcoholics Anonymous (AA), 12 Step method and encourage patients to join

AA or similar groups. Each form of treatment has its own expected outcome and the combined effect has proven to be superior to any one treatment method.

If a patient has been drinking to self medicate or to cope with stress, conventional therapy can help that person to recognize that and work with the therapist to resolve psychological issues that have prevented him or her from living a fulfilling life. This therapy will generally continue once the person has been discharged from the inpatient portion of treatment. Continued therapy can help the person to deal with any recurring issues or stress that could encourage a relapse into drinking.

Cognitive Behavior Therapy is now being used in most treatment centers because, when used in conjunction with traditional therapy, it is having remarkable success. CBT literally helps patients to recognize, avoid, and cope. This simple structure can help people learn how to avoid alcohol or drugs for the rest of their lives. Patients learn to recognize the triggers that can cause them to return to drinking, avoid any situations that might contain those triggers and what other skills they may have to cope with the original reasons for drinking. CBT is short termed, goal based and provides a person with an arsenal of tools to avoid pitfalls and traps that can encourage relapses.

A person may have started out being a warm-hearted, caring individual, but the very nature of addiction can turn the most conscientious human being into a self-centered, selfish and closed-off person. It takes practice and understanding to change these habits and group therapy can help to make these changes. Group therapy is a great method to help get patients to learn to talk about their emotions, recognize that others have similar problems, learn to listen to others and offer help and support to others in a similar situation. This form of therapy can help to bring out or bring back the parts of a person that make him or her likable and lovable.

Just about every treatment program encourages their patients to attend AA/NA meetings and will have these or similar meetings in the treatment center for patients. AA began in 1934 and is still the

#1 recovery program for alcoholics in the world today. It has weathered many discussions and has been accused as being just another addiction for already addicted people, but the truth remains that Alcoholics Anonymous has helped more people to remain sober than any other treatment, anywhere. While it may not be the right choice for everyone it is still the right choice for many and should be a part of every recovery plan.

Finally, each treatment program needs to be able to help each patient to create a Recovery Plan and a method of transitioning back into everyday life with a strong support system in place. Before you enter a treatment program, ask about the plans that are in place to help you transition back into the community and to stay sober. If you receive a vague answer about this very important aspect of recovery treatment, your best bet may be to choose a different program. Many recovering alcoholics have failed to achieve full recovery without a sound Recovery Plan in place.

The Recovery Plan is a very personal, individualized plan and a very important part of staying sober. This is the plan that the patient will ultimately create that will guide his or her alcohol free life. The next chapter in this book is devoted to the Recovery Plan, so we will leave any more to be said about it for that chapter.

7.3 Outpatient Therapy

Many alcoholics choose to avoid inpatient programs and decide to get help through an outpatient setting. This means seeing a therapist or counselor on a regular basis, sometimes taking part in group counseling sessions or family therapy and even using medication to help with abstinence. These programs are far less structured and rely on the patient to attend scheduled sessions. The person in treatment must rely on his or her self to maintain sobriety and continue with treatment as scheduled.

Outpatient therapy can offer as many different forms of therapy as an inpatient program. These may consist of using conventional one-on-one therapy to work through the issues that may have precipitated the drinking in the first place. If the person was using alcohol to self medicate because of physical or emotional pain, the therapist will want to focus on that to make sure these issues do not bring about renewed drinking. If the person started drinking because of depression or loneliness, those too could resurface once the person is sober and he or she will have no coping mechanism for dealing with the sadness or depression. The therapist and the patient may also need to work through some of the problems that have occurred as a direct result of drinking.

Outpatient therapy often includes group therapy. Like the group therapy that occurs in the inpatient setting, groups can assist the alcoholic in beginning to reach out to others to provide and receive help and support. Learning to open up to people can help immensely in new and old relationships.

By remaining in the community during outpatient therapy, the alcoholic can begin to rebuild shattered relationships with important people in his or her life. Family or relationship therapy may help to speed up the process of relationship reconstruction. This is important to help renew or create support systems that are paramount to recovery. Friends and loved ones are vital to the recovering alcoholic.

Cognitive Behavioral Therapy (CBT) should be used to help the alcoholic to understand the triggers to drinking and the behaviors that are associated with drinking. Because the alcoholic has chosen to stay in the community where he or she has been involved in drinking, there are many painful decisions that cannot be delayed. Major life changes will be necessary in order to remain alcohol free. Old friends and acquaintances will have to be left behind if they are part of the past that made drinking possible or attractive. Just as a junky can no longer associate with others who use drugs, so the alcoholic must avoid the people he or she used to drink with if those people are still drinking. People, places and activities that have been part of the alcoholism cannot be a part of the person's new life.

The alcoholic will also need to have a strong Recovery Plan in place while still in therapy. He or she should work closely with the therapist, even while still new to therapy, to develop a plan that will help the person to remain alcohol free. Because the person will be in therapy for a period of time, this plan can be updated and refined as needed. The recovering alcoholic will have the ability to share any problems or rough areas with the therapist so that the Recovery Plan will be fine tuned once the person is on his or her own.

The recovering alcoholic should also be involved in AA. This group of people will provide an ongoing support system that is not a part of the drinking scene and can also introduce the person to many alternative activities that do not include alcohol. When attending outpatient therapy, it is very important for the alcoholic to attend as many AA meetings as possible. This may be the person's only real recovery support during the early stages of sobriety and the people at AA can offer help and encouragement during a very difficult period in a person's life.

7.4 Do It Yourself

Some alcoholics have been able to recover through no professional intervention. Because there are no official records or statistics kept on people who do not seek treatment, no one knows how many alcoholics have successfully recovered this way. There are plans and techniques that some alcoholics have used and shared with others that they have found helpful when choosing to quit drinking on their own. Hopefully, some of the following ideas can help if you are an alcoholic who has chosen to quit without professional help.

Make a strong commitment to stop drinking. As with any other program, it is only as good as your commitment to make it work. Once the alcohol has safely left your system (please see the chapter on Detox), your commitment and belief that this is the right thing to do are the only things standing between you and another drink. If you are committed to recovery, you can, indeed, make that a very realistic goal.

Get rid of all the things around you that are associated with drinking. Throw out any alcohol in your home, work or areas where you spend time. Get rid of anything like barware, signs, t-shirts with drinking logos, or any other decorations that make drinking appear attractive. Put up "no drinking" signs if you need to in order to make sure no one drinks in these areas or brings in alcohol.

Learn from your past mistakes. If you have tried to quit drinking in the past but failed, think about what triggers were responsible for your relapse. There are definitely things, places, people and situation that you will need to avoid to maintain sobriety. You need to make a list of these triggers and plan either how to avoid them entirely or how to deal with them when they occur or you come into contact with them. You will need to be prepared and vigilant for these triggers because they are often quite subtle and can trip you up if they happen at an unexpected moment.

Get as much help as possible. Ask friends and family members to help and support your decision to quit drinking. Attend AA meetings as often as possible; even if you think AA is not for you, try attending several meetings when you first stop drinking; these meetings can give you a lot of help and alternative activities to drinking. Remember: drinking has been taking up a lot of your time and you may find it difficult to come up with activities to take the place of drinking when you are first recovering.

Finally, have a carefully prepared Recover Plan. This is the outline of your life after alcoholism and is vital to your recovery. The Recovery Plan is thoroughly covered in chapter 9.

CHAPTER 8
CHANGING THE EMPHASIS FROM TREATMENT TO RECOVERY

Until recently, many programs did not place much emphasis on what happened when a person left the program and then scratched their collective heads in wonder when their patients returned, again and again, unable to remain alcohol free when away from treatment. The big question became what is a person going to do to stay sober once he or she is out of treatment? Is he or she going back into the same environment, with the same triggers, that encouraged drinking in the first place? Is there a system in place to offer help and support? Many programs used words like "follow-up care" and "support systems," but they did not seem to comprehend the very real importance of these concepts.

For years and years, Alcoholism among Native Americans was so rampant that everyone simply assumed that there was a genetic predisposition toward alcoholism in these people and that is why the rates were so high. Whether there is a genetic trait or not, there have recently been some very surprising developments in alcoholism recovery among Native Americans that defy all of the previously held beliefs. There is one particular tribe, the Shuswap, in British Columbia, that at one time had an alcoholism rate of almost 100% among its adults. Today, that same tribe has an alcoholism rate of less than 5%. These same types of results are being seen in other Native American tribes and Eskimo cultures at incredible rates. Did their genetics suddenly change?

The answer lies in a cultural shift that supports a sober lifestyle and aids its members to live and function as an active member in the community as a "well" person. The Native Americans began to recognize that their culture was suffering as much as their people and they could not expect their tribal members to thrive when their culture was crumbling around them. Members set out to make the changes the revitalized and renewed their tribal values and customs which supported sobriety and wellness. As the interest grew to repair the cultural values of the tribes, more and more tribal members got involved and started several movements that promoted these values. As the culture healed, so too did its members. Programs were started to support recovering members; Native American AA groups sprang up all over and people began to support sobriety, more and more. In the last 20 years, the rate of alcoholism among Native American people has dropped dramatically.

These findings caused a lot of leaders in the professional community to realize that something vital has been missing from conventional Alcohol and a drug addiction treatment. Treatment programs needed to devote more time and effort to helping patients make plans and lifestyle changes that would support and encourage sobriety.

American culture encourages the use of alcohol and drugs and even reinforces it. This does not mean that alcohol should be made illegal; prohibition did not work and all opiates and marijuana are illegal and that has had little effect on their use. The answer lies in developing a lifestyle that does not reinforce the use of drugs or alcohol. If no one is offering a person a drink or drinking around an alcoholic, it certainly makes remaining sober much easier and desirable. That is what a good recovery plan should provide; a plan that makes living without drugs and alcohol attractive. The Native American tribes made drinking less attractive and only allowed members who were sober to participate in high-ranking positions. The result was a rebirth of a desirable culture and lifestyle where one could feel proud of being a member of the community and proud of one's self.

It is time to start looking at ways to live a meaningful life that does not include drugs or alcohol. That is one of the things that has contributed to the high success rate of the Spiritual and Faith based programs. These programs provide their patients with a support system outside of the treatment facility. The patients walk out of the treatment center doors already being a part of a tight knit, supportive community that does not reinforce the use of drugs or alcohol. The recovering alcoholics are surrounded by an entire network of people who are willing to help their fellow parishioners to remain sober and they reward that sobriety with love and acceptance; something most alcoholics have not experienced before. It is no wonder that these faith based treatment programs have been so successful.

A person can join a church, become a volunteer, do things to help in the community, help his or her family members and friends, go back to school or make a complete career change. There are many activities and events in every community that do not encourage drinking and people who do not do drugs or drink alcohol. These are some of the things that can and should be a part of a recovery plan and it is the recovery plan that keeps a person sober.

CHAPTER 9
THE RECOVERY PLAN: LIFE
AFTER ALCOHOLISM

The Recovery Plan is the outline of how a person is going to live his or her life after alcoholism. It possesses a positive outlook with an emphasis is on wellness and thriving. The Recovery Plan contains the steps toward a future that is full of wellbeing and meaning. It is a new outlook on life that celebrates living and the possibilities that life has to offer. It goes far beyond survival to thriving. It is a document that contains hope and beauty and opens the doors to a whole new life.

Sounds pretty far-fetched, doesn't it? It is not. It can be all those things and more and so can the life you choose to live after alcoholism. If you look at the things that have made the Native Americans successful in their battle against alcoholism and what makes the faith based programs so successful, you can see there is a common thread. That thread has to do with having more meaning in life than the person had before recovery. It is in community, culture and support. People who are treated in a faith based program, leave with an entire churchful of people to support them and cherish them. Native Americans who become sober have a community a tribe to belong to and be a part of and a support system of friends and family already in place when they stop drinking or using drugs.

Most alcoholics did not become alcoholics because they were spending too much time celebrating life. If you look back on the reasons you started drinking or ask any other alcoholic why he or she started drinking the reasons generally range from depression, isolation, loneliness, and feelings of meaninglessness to boredom and just plain apathy. Something was missing from life that gave it meaning. The Recovery Plan is the plan that gives you that meaning.

When you sit down and begin to write or think about your Recovery Plan, you need to think of the things that can give you some new meaning. What the Native Americans and the Faith based programs share is the knowledge that a person needs to believe that life has meaning and is worth living and one of the ways to experience that is through a feeling of, or membership in, a community. AA is a support community, so are many church groups. There are also volunteer programs that function as communities, art councils, local government councils and organizations, and a host of groups and gatherings that are always open to new members.

Have you ever thought about changing careers or returning to school? Is there someone special in your life who needs some special thank you for all the times he or she stuck by you while you continued to be destructive? Are there old dreams that got left on the shelf, long ago? Maybe it is time to look at those dreams again and think about renewing them. There are also many new opportunities waiting for you and now is the time to investigate them. Remember that old cliché from the 60's and 70's: "Today is the first day of the rest of your life." Maybe instead of laughing at that we should embrace it. Take the lessons of the Native Americans with you; your Recover Plan really can be a whole new start to a new life.

RECAP

Alcoholism is a problem that affects over 15 million people in the US today, in one form or another. Alcohol can have severe negative effects on the human body that encompass everything from skin disorders to organ failure to death. While these are grim statistics, alcoholism continues to rise. Alcoholics frequently deny the problem exists making it difficult to get an alcoholic to seek treatment. Many alcoholics must reach a point where they finally perceive their lives as being horrid before finally admitting that they need help.

Treatment for alcoholism has undergone several major changes in the last several years. One of the key changes has been a new emphasis on the importance of recovery being obtainable and becoming the focus of treatment. The outstanding occurrences of recovery among Native American tribal people caused many alcohol treatment professionals to study the reasons the recovery rate was so high. They realized that the people who focused on an enriched life after alcoholism and a recovery plan that included active involvement in a supportive community were less likely to return to drinking. Using this model, alcoholism treatment now includes a recovery plan with an emphasis on improving and adding meaning to a recovering alcoholic's life. This approach is proving to be quite successful in treating alcoholism and drug addiction.

Limited Bonus

Thanks a lot for reading this book. If you like this book, please leave me a review on Amazon.

Moreover, quick action takers get rewarded !

Get your bonus using this following url: http://eepurl.com/rdVYb and

1. Get my next book on Amazon for FREE !

2. Receive useful references (from the Internet)